INSTRUCTOR'S RESOURCE MANUAL

Evelyn E. Kelly
with Jamie Barrett

ALONG THESE LINES

WRITING SENTENCES AND PARAGRAPHS

John S. Biays

Carol Wershoven

PRENTICE HALL, UPPER SADDLE RIVER, NEW JERSEY 07458

©2001 by PRENTICE-HALL, INC.
PEARSON EDUCATION
Upper Saddle River, New Jersey 07458

10 9 8 7 6 5 4 3 2 1

ISBN 0-13-091279-4

Printed in the United States of America

CONTENTS

CHAPTER ONE OVERVIEW

Chapter One focuses on the make-up of the simple sentence, beginning with verb and subject recognition. There are two categories of verbs: **action verbs** and **being verbs**. Exercises in this section cover recognizing the two types of verbs in sentences. An infobox provides a list of common **helping verbs** which may be used in conjunction with action and being verbs. Exercises in recognizing the main verb and helping verbs in sentences and writing sentences that contain helping verbs reinforce the discussion. The lesson cautions students to look for more than one main verb in a sentence and provides related practice exercises. An excerpt from "The Tell-Tale Heart" allows additional practice in verb recognition.

Next, the lesson addresses subject recognition. Students learn the technique of asking a question, "Who or what does the action or expresses the state of being?" The answer is the subject of the sentence or clause. Students must also look for more than one subject in a sentence, just as they do with the verbs. Practice exercises in recognizing and adding subjects follow.

After subject recognition, the lesson addresses **prepositions** and **prepositional phrases**. A second infobox provides a list of common prepositions. Students learn to identify prepositions and prepositional phrases to avoid confusion when finding the subjects of sentences. Practice exercises allow students to identify prepositional phrases in sentences and create sentences that contain prepositional phrases.

The next area of discussion concerns **word order**. Several situations affect simple word order, subject first and then the verb:

1) prepositional phrases

2) sentences that begin with *There is/are* or *Here is/are*

3) questions.

Each area contains exercises in recognizing the subject and verb.

Chapter One also includes a discussion of words that are misidentified as verbs or main verbs. **Adverbs** look like verbs and are often close to verbs, but they are not verbs. Verb forms such as **-ing verbs** and **infinitives** cannot stand alone as main verbs. The pronoun test allows students to differentiate between main verbs and adverbs and verb forms that cannot be main verbs. Exercises in this section provide practice in correcting problems with infinitives and -ing verbs.

Chapter One concludes with comprehensive exercises in recognizing subjects and verbs and creating sentences based on the rules covered in the chapter.

Additional Collaborative Exercise for Chapter One

Provide groups of students with newspaper or magazine articles. Have them identify the subject and verb in each sentence, paying special attention to prepositional phrases, infinitives, -ing verbs and adverbs.

CHAPTER TWO OVERVIEW

Chapter Two instructs students in combining simple sentences using **coordination**, joining equals. There are three options for combining simple sentences using coordination:

Option 1: Using a comma and a **coordinating conjunction**. These are easy to learn by using the

acronym fanboys:　,for
　　　　　　　　　,and
　　　　　　　　　,nor
　　　　　　　　　,but
　　　　　　　　　,or
　　　　　　　　　,yet
　　　　　　　　　,so

Three exercises in punctuating **compound sentences** using coordinating conjunctions follow.

Option 2: Using a semicolon. A semicolon may be used to join two simple sentences that are

related in their ideas.

This section includes practice exercises in recognizing compound sentences and adding semicolons.

Option 3: Using a semicolon and a **conjunctive adverb**. An infobox provides a list of common

conjunctive adverbs. The lesson explains the correct punctuation of conjunctive

adverbs when joining compound sentences.

Exercises provide additional practice in recognizing and punctuating compound sentences with conjunctive adverbs and writing sentences with conjunctive adverbs.

Chapter Two concludes with exercises using all three options to combine simple sentences.

Additional Collaborative Exercises for Chapter Two

1. Have students create a list of simple sentences on a specific subject. Next, have them

   combine the sentences using coordination.

2. Working in groups, students will rewrite an article from a newspaper or magazine using the

   three coordination options. Each new article can be shared with the rest of the class.

CHAPTER THREE OVERVIEW

The focus of Chapter Three is avoiding **run-on sentences (fused sentence)** and **comma splices**. A run-on sentence error occurs when two independent clauses are run together without the necessary punctuation. There are two steps for correcting run-on sentence errors:

1) Check for two independent clauses.

2) Check that the clauses are separated by either a coordinating conjunction and a comma or by a semicolon.

Exercises in correcting run-on sentence errors reinforce the lesson.

A comma splice error occurs when a comma is used for punctuation when a semicolon should be used. When joining two independent clauses without a coordinating conjunction, a semicolon must be used, not just a comma. There are two steps for correcting comma splices:

1) Check for two independent clauses.

2) Check that the clauses are separated by a coordinating conjunction. If they are, then a comma before the coordinating conjunction is sufficient. If they are not separated by a coordinating conjunction, there is a comma splice. Correct it by changing the comma to a semicolon.

Exercises in correcting comma splices provide additional practice.

Chapter Three concludes with comprehensive exercises on correcting problems with run-on sentences and comma splices.

Additional Collaborative Exercise for Chapter Three

Working in groups, students will create a list of compound sentences. Next, they will rewrite them, removing the commas and semicolons. These can serve as additional practice exercises for other groups to correct.

CHAPTER FOUR OVERVIEW

Chapter Four offers more options for combining simple sentences. The lesson covers **subordination**. Students use **dependent clauses** to begin or end sentences. A dependent clause has a subject and verb but does not make sense by itself

Adding a **subordinating conjunction** or a **relative pronoun** to an independent clause changes it to a dependent clause. An infobox provides a list of subordinating conjunctions and relative pronouns. A sentence with one independent clause and two or more dependent clauses is a **complex sentence**.

Next, students learn to punctuate complex sentences. If the dependent clause is at the beginning of the sentence, a comma goes after the clause. If the dependent clause is at the end of the sentence, the clause needs no comma.

Practice exercises in this chapter cover punctuating complex sentences, combining sentences, and creating complex sentences from dependent clauses.

Additional Collaborative Exercise for Chapter Four

Provide students with a list of simple sentences. Have them turn each sentence into a complex sentence, paying special attention to punctuation.

CHAPTER FIVE OVERVIEW

Chapter Five reminds students of the importance of combining sentences to avoid a choppy writing style. **Sentence variety** involves mixing long and short sentences. The chapter provides a chart that contains the five options for combining sentences using coordination and subordination. Practice exercises provide additional practice in combining simple sentences, creating a text, editing paragraphs with compound and complex sentences, and combining sentences in a paragraph.

Additional Collaborative Exercise for Chapter Five

Working in groups, students combine two simple sentences using all five options. Answers may be shared with other groups.

CHAPTER SIX OVERVIEW

Chapter Six explains how to avoid **sentence fragments**, a group of words that looks like a sentence and is punctuated like a sentence, but is not a sentence. There are two steps for recognizing fragments:

1) Look for a subject and a verb.

2) If there is a subject and a verb, check for a complete statement.

The lesson also cautions students to look for fragments formed with -ing verbs and **infinitives**, *to* plus a verb. Neither can be the main verb in a sentence. Groups of words beginning with *also, especially, except, for example, for instance, in addition*, and *such as* need subjects and verbs.

An infobox provides a list of common subordinating conjunctions and relative pronouns. After checking for a subject and a verb, students should check to see if the clause begins with a subordinating conjunction or a relative pronoun. These clauses are **dependent-clause fragments**; they do not make a complete statement.

Exercises in this section provide practice in checking groups of words for subjects and verbs and checking for dependent-clause fragments.

Next, the lesson addresses correcting sentence fragments. If the group of words lacks a subject or verb, students add what is missing. To correct dependent-clause fragments, students can remove the subordinating conjunction or add an independent clause to the dependent clause. Sometimes students can correct a sentence fragment by adding it to the sentence that comes before or after it.

Chapter Six concludes with exercises in correcting fragments and editing a paragraph with fragments.

Additional Collaborative Exercise for Chapter Six

Students often create sentence-fragment errors when writing because sentence fragments appear often in informal speech. Have students record a conversation between two or three friends. Instruct students to write down all of the sentence fragments used in the conversation and correct each fragment using the methods discussed in class.

CHAPTER SEVEN OVERVIEW

The focus of Chapter Seven is using **parallelism**, balance in sentences. To achieve parallelism in sentences, students must give similar points a similar structure. There are two steps in checking a sentence for parallel structure:

1) Look for the list in the sentence.

2) Give the parts of the list a similar structure.

In order to make sentences parallel, students must sometimes add words to the sentence. Chapter six includes excerpts of two famous speeches which contain parallel structure. Exercises in this section provide practice in revising sentences for parallelism, writing sentences with parallelism, and editing paragraphs for parallelism.

Additional Collaborative Exercise for Chapter Seven

Instruct students to create a tedious job with numerous responsibilities. Have them categorize the duties of the job and then create sentences that list the duties. Advise students to use a different parallel structure for each sentence.

CHAPTER EIGHT OVERVIEW

Chapter eight focuses on **adjectives** and **adverbs**. Adjectives describe nouns or pronouns. An adjective usually comes before the word it describes, but it can also come after a being verb. Practice exercises in recognizing adjectives follow the discussion.

The next section addresses the **comparative form** (comparing two persons or things) and the **superlative form** (comparing three or more persons or things). The lesson supplies the rules for creating these forms:

1) For most one-syllable adjectives, add -*er* to form the comparative and -*est* to form the superlative.

2) For longer adjectives, use *more* to form the comparative and *most* to form the superlative. Chapter Eight also includes some irregular forms of adjectives. Exercises in selecting the correct adjective form and writing sentences with adjectives complete the lesson.

The second half of the chapter addresses adverb use. Adverbs describe verbs, adjectives, and other verbs. After examples of adverb usage in sentences are practice exercises in recognizing adverbs and writing sentences with adverbs.

The lesson cautions against common errors when using adjectives and adverbs:

1) Do not use an adjective when you need an adverb.

2) Do not confuse *good* and *well* or *bad* and *badly*.

3) Do not use *more* + -*er* or *most* + -*est*.

4) Use *than*, not *then*, in comparisons.

Students also learn when to use a comma between adjectives. To determine when a comma is needed, there are two tests:

1) Put *and* between the adjectives. If the sentence still makes sense, put a comma between the adjectives.

2) Reverse the order of the adjectives. If the sentence still makes sense, put a comma between

the adjectives.

Chapter Eight concludes with comprehensive exercises in using adjectives and adverbs and editing a paragraph for errors in adjectives and adverbs.

Additional Collaborative Exercise for Chapter Eight

Provide groups of students with a list of sentences that contain no adjectives. Have them add two adjectives for each noun and then add two adverbs to each new sentence. Sentences can be read aloud.

CHAPTER NINE OVERVIEW

Chapter Nine addresses problems with **modifiers**. Modifiers are words, phrases or clauses that describe (modify) something in a sentence. Students practice recognizing modifiers in sentences and in an excerpt from a newspaper article. There are three steps in checking for sentence errors with modifiers:

1) Find the modifier.

2) Check to see if the modifier has something to modify.

3) Check to see if the modifier is as close as possible to the word, phrase or clause it modifies.

One form of modifier problem is the **misplaced modifier**. A misplaced modifier error occurs when the modifier is not where it should be in the sentence. The lesson cautions students to be especially careful with the placement of words such as *almost, even, exactly, hardly, just, merely, nearly, only, scarcely,* and *simply* to avoid writing confusing sentences.

A second error with modifiers is the **dangling modifier**, a modifier that has nothing to modify. An infobox reviews the steps for checking for modifier problems along with ways to correct them:

1) If a modifier is in the wrong place, put it as close as possible to the word, phrase, or clause it modifies.

2) If a modifier has nothing to modify, add or change words so it has something to modify.

The lesson includes several practice exercises in correcting misplaced and dangling modifier errors.

Additional Collaborative Exercise for Chapter Nine

Provide groups of students with a list of sentences. Have them create modifiers that can be placed in the sentences. Next, students will exchange the lists of modifiers and each group will create new sentences using the modifiers, paying careful attention to correct placement.

CHAPTER TEN OVERVIEW

Chapter Ten introduces the four main verb forms. **Verbs** are words that show some kind of action or being. Verbs also tell about time. The time of a verb is called its **tense**.

Students learn to differentiate between the Standard English of college, business, and professional environments and the nonstandard forms used in everyday conversation.

Chapter Ten discusses two verb tenses:

1) **Present tense**--For present tense, use an *-s* or *-es* ending on the verb only when the subject is *he*, *she*, or *it*.

Exercises provide practice in selecting the right verb in present tense, writing sentences with verbs in the present tense, and revising a paragraph for errors in the present tense.

2) **Past Tense**--Form the past tense of most verbs by adding *-d* or *-ed* to the verb.

This section includes exercises in writing the correct form of the past tense, writing sentences with verbs in present and past tense, and revising a paragraph by changing present tense verbs to past tense.

The four main forms of a verb are the present tense, the past tense, **the present participle**, and **the past participle**. The four forms may be used alone or with helping verbs:

1) Use the present form for the present tense.

2) Use the past form for the past tense.

3) Use the present participle or *-ing form* with helping verbs.

4) Use the past participle with the helping verbs *have*, *has*, or *had*.

Practice exercises in writing sentences with the four main forms of a verb follow the discussion.

The next section of Chapter Ten focuses on the irregular verbs *be*, *have*, and *do*. Irregular verbs do not follow the same rules for creating verb forms that regular verbs do. Several exercises in choosing the correct form of *be*, *have*, and *do* in the present and past tense provide additional practice. The lesson includes an extensive list of irregular verbs in

13

present, past, and past participle forms along with exercises in choosing the correct form of the verbs in sentences and paragraphs.

Additional Collaborative Exercise for Chapter Ten

Provide students with an excerpt from a short story. Instruct them to change all of the verbs to one or more of the four verb forms.

CHAPTER ELEVEN OVERVIEW

Chapter Eleven provides more discussion on verb tenses. The main verb forms (present, past, present participle, and past participle) can be combined with helping verbs to create more verb tenses. An infobox lists common helping verbs which change their form, depending on the subject.

Fixed-form helping verbs always keep the same form regardless of the subject. A second infobox lists fixed-form helping verbs. The lesson gives special emphasis to the verbs *can* and *could* and *will* and *would*:

1) *Can* is used to show present tense.

2) *Could* is used to show past tense.

   Could is also used to show a possibility or a wish.

3) *Will* points to the future from the present.

4) *Would* points to the future from the past.

   Would is also used to show a possibility or a wish.

Practice exercises allow students to recognize helping verbs in sentences and select *can* or *could*; *will* or *would* in sentences.

Next, the lesson introduces the **present progressive tense**. The present progressive tense uses the present participle (the *-ing* form of the verb) plus some form of *to be*. The present progressive tense shows that the action is happening right now and should not be confused with present tense. The present progressive can also show future time. An exercise in distinguishing between the present tense and the present progressive follows.

Chapter Eleven also explains the **past progressive tense**. The past progressive tense uses the present participle (the *-ing* form of the verb) plus a past form of *to be*. This verb shows that something was in progress. This section of the lesson includes an exercise in distinguishing between the past tense and the past progressive tense.

15

The chapter next discusses the **present perfect tense**. The present perfect tense is made up of the past participle form of a verb plus *have* or *has* as a helping verb. The present perfect tense shows that an action started in the past and is still going on in the present.

The next area of discussion is the **past perfect tense**. The past perfect tense consists of the past participle form of the verb plus *had* as a helping verb. Past perfect tense shows when two or more events happened in the past but at different times. An exercise in distinguishing between past and past perfect tenses reinforces the discussion.

Chapter Eleven also includes reminders about verb usage:

1) Write *used to* instead of *use to*.

2) Use *supposed to* instead of *suppose to.*

3) Use *could have*, *should have*, and *would have* instead of *could of, should of* or *would of.*

4) Use *had* instead of *would have* when writing about something that might have been possible but did not happen.

Chapter Eleven concludes with exercises in editing paragraphs for verb errors and writing sentences with correct verb forms.

Additional Collaborative Exercise for Chapter Eleven

Working in groups, students will write sentences in one tense and then change them to another tense: present tense to present progressive tense

past tense to past progressive tense/ present perfect tense/ past perfect tense

CHAPTER TWELVE OVERVIEW

The focus of Chapter Twelve is **verb consistency and voice**. Consistency of verb tense is staying in one tense unless there is a reason to change tense. Exercises allow additional practice in correcting sentences and editing paragraphs for consistency of tense.

The second half of the chapter focuses on voice. Verbs have two voices:

1) **Active voice**- the subject of the sentence is doing something.

2) **Passive voice**- something is done to the subject. Passive voice can make sentences wordy, it can slow them down, and it can make them boring or confusing; therefore, students should avoid the passive voice unless it is necessary to use it. The passive voice is used when it is not known who did something. Students must also avoid shifts in verb voice.

Exercises in this section involve changing verbs from passive voice to active voice and correcting shifts in voice. A comprehensive exercise in editing a paragraph for errors in consistent verb tense and voice concludes the chapter.

Additional Collaborative Exercise for Chapter Twelve

Provide groups of students with different magazine or newspaper articles. Instruct them to change the sentences in the articles to passive voice. Have someone read the new articles aloud. Students should note the change in the length of the articles. Some will also be confusing. The rewritten articles can also be exchanged, and each group can change the sentences back to active voice for additional practice.

CHAPTER THIRTEEN OVERVIEW

The topic of Chapter Thirteen is **subject-verb agreement**. Subjects and verbs must agree in number. The lesson reminds students that a regular verb has an -*s* ending in third person singular. If a pronoun is used as the subject of a sentence, it must agree in number with the verb.

Sometimes it is difficult to find the subject of a sentence or determine if the subject is singular or plural:

1) Prepositional phrases should be eliminated to find the subject of a sentence. The lesson includes exercises in finding the subject and verb of a sentence by recognizing prepositional phrases.

2) Changed word order can cause problems in finding the subject of a sentence because the subject does nor come before the verb. Changed word order occurs in questions and sentences beginning with *Here is/ are* and *There is/ are*. This section also includes exercises to reinforce the lesson.

3) A **compound subject** is two or more subjects joined by *and, or,* or *nor*. Students must remember to check for compound subjects in changed word order. When subjects are joined by *and*, they are usually plural. When compound subjects are joined by *or, either... or, neither ...nor,* or *not only...but also*, the verb form agrees with the subject closest to the verb. This section includes an exercise in making subjects and verbs agree with compound subjects and a review in recognizing subjects and verbs.

4) **Indefinite pronouns** always take a singular verb even if the pronoun seems plural. An infobox lists common indefinite pronouns. Exercises in making subjects and verbs agree using indefinite pronouns complete the lesson.

5) **Collective nouns** refer to more than one person or thing. An infobox provides a list of common collective nouns. Collective nouns usually take a singular verb. They take a plural verb only when the members of the group are acting individually and not as a unit. This

section also includes a practice exercise.

Chapter Thirteen concludes with a review of the rules for subject-verb agreement and a comprehensive exercise.

Additional Collaborative Exercise for Chapter Thirteen

Working in groups, students will create a list of sentences that begin with pronouns, prepositional phrases, changed word order, compound subjects, or collective nouns. Next, have them rewrite each sentence, removing the verb or providing two choices (one incorrect). These will be shared with other groups and used as practice exercises.

CHAPTER FOURTEEN OVERVIEW

The subject of Chapter Fourteen is **pronoun agreement and reference.** A **pronoun** is a word that substitutes for a noun. A pronoun's **antecedent** is the word or word it replaces. Students practice identifying the antecedents of pronouns in sentences.

A pronoun must agree in number with its antecedent. Singular antecedents must have singular pronouns, and plural antecedents must have plural pronouns. The lesson discusses special problems with agreement:

1) **Indefinite pronouns**--Indefinite pronouns are always singular. When an indefinite pronoun is the antecedent, the pronoun that replaces it must be singular. An infobox provides a list of indefinite pronouns. Students also learn to avoid sexism in writing. This section of the lesson provides exercises in pronoun agreement with indefinite pronouns.

2) **Collective nouns**--Most of the time, collective nouns take singular verbs because the group is acting as a unit. Collective nouns take a plural pronoun only when the members of the group are acting individually and not as a unit. An infobox lists common collective nouns. Exercises provide practice in making pronouns and antecedents agree with collective nouns as antecedents.

The second half of the chapter focuses on pronoun reference:

1) A pronoun must have one clear antecedent.

2) A pronoun must have an antecedent..

Students practice rewriting and revising sentences for clear reference of pronouns and editing a paragraph for errors in pronoun reference.

Additional Collaborative Exercise for Chapter Fourteen

Provide groups of students with excerpts from a short story. Instruct them to identify pronouns and their antecedents.

CHAPTER FIFTEEN OVERVIEW

Chapter Fifteen continues the discussion on pronoun usage. The focus of this chapter is **pronoun consistency and case**. The lesson explains first, second, and third person point of view and the pronoun form used with each point of view. When writing, students should be consistent with pronoun form. Practice exercises in pronoun consistency in sentences follow the discussion.

The next section addresses pronoun case:

1) **Subjective case** -- used when the pronoun serves as the subject of a sentence or clause.

2) **Objective case** -- used when the pronoun is the object of a verb or the object of a preposition.

3) **Possessive case**--used when a pronoun shows ownership.

A practice exercise in choosing the correct case of pronouns reinforces the lesson.

The chapter also addresses common errors in choosing pronoun case:

1) Students learn to isolate the pronoun in a related group of words to determine the correct pronoun case.

2) *Between* is a preposition. Pronouns that follow it are objects of the preposition, so they must be objective case.

3) *Myself* cannot be a replacement for *I* or *me*.

Chapter Fifteen concludes with exercises on choosing the right case of pronouns, creating a text on pronoun case, and editing a paragraph for pronoun case.

Additional Collaborative Exercise for Chapter Fifteen

Divide students into three groups. Using the infobox on page 173, assign each group a pronoun case. Groups will create six sentences using each pronoun on the list. Sentences can be shared. For additional practice, assign each group a different case and repeat the exercise.

CHAPTER SIXTEEN OVERVIEW

Chapter Sixteen covers the basic rules of punctuation:

1) The **period**--Use a period at the end of a sentence that makes a statement and after abbreviations.

2) The **question mark**--Use a question mark after a direct question.

3) The **semicolon**--Use a semicolon to join two independent clauses and when a list contains commas and the items on the list need to be clarified.

4) The **comma**--There are four main ways to use a comma:

   a) Comma as lister: Commas separate items (words, phrases, or clauses) in a list.

   b) Comma as linker: Use a comma and a coordinating conjunction to link two independent clauses.

   c) Comma as introducer: Use a comma after introductory words, phrases, or clauses in a sentence.

   d) Comma as inserter: Use commas around words or phrases that are not necessary in a sentence.

In addition to the four main ways to use commas, there are four minor ways:

   e) Use commas to set off a direct question from the rest of the sentence.

   f) Use commas with dates and addresses.

   g) Use commas in numbers.

   h) Use commas for clarity.

5) The **apostrophe**-- Use the apostrophe in contractions, to show possession, for special uses of time, the creation of a plural for numbers mentioned as numbers, letters mentioned as letters, and words that normally do not have plurals.

6) The **colon**-- Use a colon at the end of a complete sentence to introduce a list or explanation and to introduce a long quotation.

7) The **exclamation mark**--Use an exclamation mark at the end of a sentence that expresses strong emotion.

8) The **dash**--Use the dash to set off words in a sentence. The dash is somewhat dramatic.

9) **Parentheses**--Use parentheses to set off words in a sentence.

10) The **hyphen**--Use the hyphen to join two or more descriptive words that act as a single word.

11) **Quotation marks**--Use quotation marks for direct quotations, for the titles of short works, for special words in a sentence, and for a quotation within a quotation.

12) **Capital letters**--(The lesson lists numerous uses)

13) **Abbreviations**--Use common abbreviations such as Mr., Mrs., Ms., Jr., Sr., and Dr. when they appear with a proper name. Use abbreviations for references to time and for organizations widely known by initials.

Chapter Sixteen includes individual exercises for each form of punctuation. The chapter concludes with three comprehensive punctuation exercises.

Additional Collaborative Exercise for Chapter Sixteen

Divide students into groups. Have them find each form of punctuation in newspaper and magazine articles. Students can compete to see which group completes the task first.

CHAPTER SEVENTEEN OVERVIEW

Chapter Seventeen assists students in becoming better spellers. First, students differentiate between **vowels** (*a, e, i, o, u* and sometimes *y*) and **consonants** (all the other letters).

The chapter introduces five spelling rules:

1) doubling a final consonant

2) dropping the final *e*

3) changing the final *y* to *i*

4) adding *s* or *es*

5) using *ie* or *ei*

Each section includes practice exercises. Two comprehensive exercises provide additional practice.

The second half of Chapter Seventeen addresses words that should be combined to make one word or spelled as two words. The spelling of some words depends on their meaning. The chapter concludes with an extensive list of commonly misspelled words.

Additional Collaborative Exercise for Chapter Seventeen

Divide students into pairs. Instruct them to give each other spelling tests on words formed from the spelling rules and the list of commonly misspelled words in the chapter. They can then pay specific attention to problem areas /words.

CHAPTER EIGHTEEN OVERVIEW

Chapter Eighteen provides an extensive list of words that sound alike or look alike. Each grouping includes a definition of each word and uses each word in a sentence. Exercises focusing on the words appear at intervals in the list. Students practice selecting the correct word in sentences, creating sentences, and editing paragraphs for words that sound alike or look alike.

Additional Collaborative Exercise for Chapter Eighteen

Divide students into pairs. One student will read a sentence from the lesson The other student will decide which form of the words that sound alike or look alike to use. Instruct students to alternate roles and pay special attention to trouble areas.

CHAPTER NINETEEN OVERVIEW

Chapter Nineteen addresses the correct use of **prepositions**. Prepositions are usually short words that often signal a kind of position, possession, or other relationship. Prepositions show time and indicate place. They also combine with other words to show expressions. Chapter Nineteen provides an extensive list of prepositions with definitions. The lesson also incorporates each preposition into a sentence.

Exercises in the chapter provide practice in choosing the correct preposition in sentences, writing sentences using expressions with prepositions, and recognizing prepositional phrases in a famous speech.

Additional Collaborative Exercise for Chapter Nineteen

Provide groups of students with a list of short simple sentences. Instruct them to add expressions with prepositions to create new sentences.

CHAPTER TWENTY OVERVIEW

The paragraph-writing process begins in Chapter Twenty. A **paragraph** is a group of sentences focusing on one idea or one point. The lesson focuses on the **thought lines** for creating a seven to twelve sentence paragraph.

Initially, students learn the processes of **freewriting**, **brainstorming**, and **keeping a journal**. Freewriting involves writing without stopping, allowing ideas to flow. Brainstorming differs from freewriting in that the writer pauses to ask questions that will lead to new ideas. A journal is a notebook of personal writing. It is a good way to practice writing and a source of ideas for writing. A paragraph develops from a specific idea that can be developed into a topic. Freewriting, brainstorming, and journals generate specific ideas. Practice exercises in this section allow students to brainstorm questions and answers, find specific ideas in a list, and find specific ideas and topics in freewriting.

Once students choose an idea, it is developed with ideas. Students add details by checking for ideas that fit the one picked, asking more questions and using the answers as details, and listing any new ideas that may be connected to the first idea.

The next step is to focus the topic and ideas around a point. Students can mark a list of related topics or map related ideas. **Mapping** means to cluster related ideas into separate lists. The exercises in this section provide practice in grouping related items in lists of details.

The discussion moves on to forming a **topic sentence** that summarizes the details of a paragraph. Topic sentences do not announce and should not be too broad or too narrow to develop in one paragraph. Practice exercises reinforce each discussion. Additional exercises allow students to recognize and write good topic sentences.

Additional Collaborative Exercise for Chapter Twenty

Students will do a freewriting exercise and then divide into groups. Instruct students to check each other's writing for ideas that can be developed into topic sentences. A discussion follows.

CHAPTER TWENTY-ONE OVERVIEW

Chapter Twenty-one continues the paragraph-writing process began in Chapter Twenty. After writing the topic sentence, students begin working on the **outline**, a plan that helps the writer stay focused.

The initial step is to check the list of details that support the topic sentence. Students learn to add details when there are not enough and eliminate details that do not relate to the topic sentence. Practice exercises in adding and eliminating details reinforce the lesson.

Once the list is complete, students can develop the outline of the paragraph. An infobox offers a checklist for an outline:

1) **Unity**--Make sure all the details relate to the topic sentence.

2) **Support**--Make sure there are enough supporting details.

3) **Coherence**--Make sure the ideas are listed in the right order.

Next, the lesson addresses the order of details. The logical order depends on the subject of the paragraph. If writing about an event, students might use **time order** (such as telling what happened first, second, etc.); if they are arguing some point, they might use **emphatic order** (such as saving the most convincing idea for last); if students are describing something, they might use **space order** (such as describing from left to right or from top to bottom). Practice exercises in this section cover putting details in the right order.

The final section of Chapter Twenty-one discusses the placement of the topic sentence in the paragraph. The topic sentence can be placed at the beginning, in the middle, or at the end of a paragraph. The lesson concludes with exercises on identifying the topic sentence in paragraphs.

Additional Collaborative Exercises for Chapter Twenty-one

Divide students into groups. Instruct each group to write a short narrative and then scramble the sentences. Groups will exchange the scrambled sentences and practice putting them back in the correct order.

CHAPTER TWENTY-TWO OVERVIEW

Chapter Twenty-two discusses the **rough lines** stage of the writing process during which the paragraph is drafted, revised, edited, and drafted again. Students may write several **drafts** or versions of the paragraphs. **Revising** the draft means rewriting it to change the structure, the order of the sentences, and the content. **Editing** refers to making changes in the choice of words, in the selection of details, in the punctuation, and in the patterns and kinds of sentences. In this phase, students add **transitions** (words, phrases, or sentences that link ideas).

The lesson provides students with a checklist of questions that should be applied to the draft concerning unity, support, coherence, style, grammar, and transitions. Students practice revising a draft for unity, support, coherence, and style. Additional exercises provide practice in revising a draft by combining sentences, correcting run-on sentences and correcting sentence fragments.

Additional Collaborative Exercise for Chapter Twenty-Two

Divide students into pairs. Students will read their partner's draft and offer suggestion on revising and editing.

CHAPTER TWENTY-THREE OVERVIEW

Chapter Twenty-three focuses on preparing the final draft of a paragraph. When polishing and proofreading the final draft, students check for errors in word choice, spelling, punctuation, and mechanics. Each paragraph should also have a final statement. Practice exercises allow students to correct errors in the final draft of a paragraph.

If required, students will give the paragraph a title. The title should be short and fit the paragraph's subject.

An infobox reviews the steps of the writing process: thought lines, outlines, rough lines and final lines. A paragraph with each phase highlighted reinforces the lesson.

In Chapter Twenty-three, students are introduced to the peer review form.

Additional Collaborative Exercise for Chapter Twenty-three

Provide students with paragraph excerpts from magazine articles or short stories. Working in groups, students can practice creating a title for each paragraph.

CHAPTER TWENTY-FOUR OVERVIEW

Chapter Twenty-four addresses **coherence** (clear and logical organization) and **unity** (the writing makes a point, and all the details relate to the point). Students learn to check for coherence and unity during all stages of the writing process. Exercises in this section involve finding topics in freewriting and brainstorming for details.

Once students create a list of details, they group the details and select a logical order which will give the paragraph coherence. To give the paragraph unity, students next give the paragraph a point--a topic sentence. Exercises provide practice in grouping details, deciding on a logical order, and creating topic sentences.

Students also focus on coherence and unity in the outlines stage of the writing process. Details that do not fit the topic sentence should not be in the outline. Details in the outline should follow a logical order. Exercises provide additional practice.

In the rough lines phase, students check the draft for coherence and unity by following a checklist of questions. They should stick to the point, take out ideas that do not fit, add ideas that make the point easier to follow, change word order if necessary, and link ideas using transitions. An infobox provides a list of common transitions and their uses. Exercises in this section involve recognizing transitions, adding appropriate transitions, using transitions, and correcting errors in final lines. The peer review form concerns coherence and unity in a paragraph.

Chapter Twenty-four concludes with three articles: "Binge Nights: The Emergency on Campus," "The Baby Myna," and "I Fell in Love, or My Hormones Awakened." At the end of each reading are exercises related to coherence and unity and writing from reading.

Additional Collaborative Exercises for Chapter Twenty-Four

Provide groups of students with newspaper or magazine articles. Have them decide the logical order and mark all transitions. Sentences in the articles may also be scrambled, and students can practice putting them back in the correct order.

CHAPTER TWENTY-FIVE OVERVIEW

The focus of Chapter Twenty-five is **support** and details. Support means that the writer says enough about the point and includes enough specific detail. Students check for sufficient support and specific detail during each stage of the writing process. Exercises cover identifying topics and developing ideas by brainstorming. Students also practice grouping details and writing topic sentences.

Once the students create topic sentences and list and group details, they can create outlines. Students check the outline for support and detail. Practice exercises cover using specific words, finding specific words to match general terms, adding details to an outline, and revising an outline.

Once the outline is completed, students write first drafts of their paragraphs. The lesson provides a checklist for adding support and details to the draft of a paragraph.

One way to make details vivid is to use **sense words**. Sense words are words that relate to the five senses. An infobox assists students in using sense words. Exercises provide practice in interviewing for specific answers, using sense words, brainstorming sense words for a paragraph, and revising for specific details or sense words.

The final phase is adding support and details to the final draft. In this section, students practice correcting errors in the final lines. The peer review form in this section focuses on support and details.

Chapter Twenty-five concludes with three articles: "I Wish," "Death Row," and "A Different Mirror."

Additional Collaborative Exercise for Chapter Twenty-five

Give students an excerpt from a newspaper, magazine article, or a short story. Instruct them to enhance the article by adding specific words.

CHAPTER TWENTY-SIX OVERVIEW

Chapter Twenty-six addresses writing from reading. Before they begin, students must have a certain **attitude** which involves thinking of what they read as half of a conversation. Students must, therefore, respond to the writer's opinions or ideas and agree, disagree, or question them.

The initial stage of writing from reading is **prereading**. Prereading means to scan the article for length, subheadings, charts, graphs, photographs or illustrations, introductory material, and title. The lesson includes a prereading checklist. It also helps to ask questions before reading.

The second step of writing from reading is **reading**. Students should try to get a sense of the whole piece by reading with questions in mind. They should reread confusing parts and search for unfamiliar words in the vocabulary list.

The next phase of writing from reading is **rereading with a pen or pencil**. In this phase, students make notes or write about what they read. Students will develop personal systems that determine what they write during the rereading phase.

The lesson uses the article "Part-Time Job May Do Teenagers More Harm Than Good" to demonstrate each phase of writing from reading.

A **summary** is one type of writing that can be done after reading. A summary of a reading gives the main ideas in a brief form and in the student's own words. It includes the writer's main ideas, the ideas used to explain the main ideas, and some examples or details. Exercises in this section cover marking a list of ideas and finding the main idea for a summary.

Chapter Twenty-six also discusses writing a **reaction** to a reading and an **agree or disagree paragraph**. A reaction is a writing about some idea from the reading. An agree or disagree paragraph agrees or disagrees with a point in the reading selection. To do these assignments, students apply the four phases of the paragraph-writing process.

The final section of the lesson focuses on writing for an **essay test**, writing about an assigned reading from memory. Before the test, students should apply the steps of reading.

Shortly before the test, they should review the marked reading assignment. During the test, applying the stages of the writing process should bring desired results. Students also need to organize their time, devoting a certain amount to each stage depending on the amount of time scheduled for the test.

Chapter Twenty-six includes the articles "New Directions," and "Home Away From Home" along with writing from reading exercises.

Additional Collaborative Exercise for Chapter Twenty-Six

Give groups of students an article and have them apply the writing from reading process. You may choose essays from the textbook. Instruct them to compare the items they noticed during the prereading phase and the items marked during the rereading phase. A discussion follows.

APPENDIX OVERVIEW

The Appendix of <u>Along These Lines</u> focuses on grammar for ESL students. It begins with nouns and articles. **Nouns** name a person, place, or thing and can be divided into two categories:

1) **Count nouns**--persons, places, or things that can be counted.

2) **Noncount nouns**--things that cannot be counted.

Related exercises follow. A helpful hint is to place the words *much* in front of the noun. If it is correct, then the noun is a noncount noun.

Articles point out nouns and can also be divided into two categories:

1) **Indefinite**--*a, an.* Use *a* in front of consonant sounds; use *an* before vowel sounds. Do
   not use *a* or *an* with noncount nouns.

2) **Definite**--*the.* Use *the* before both singular and plural count nouns whose specific identity is known to the reader. Use *the* before noncount nouns only when they are specifically identified. This section contains exercises using *a, an,* and *the* in sentences and correcting a paragraph with errors in articles.

Next, the lesson discusses **pronouns** used as subjects. A pronoun is a word that takes the place of a noun. All sentences or dependent clauses have a subject. The lesson also cautions students not to repeat the subject. A practice exercise in correcting errors with subjects reinforces the lesson.

Verbs are the focus of the final section of the Appendix. A sentence or dependent clause must have a verb. Past tense verbs in the third person singular require the *-s* ending. The past participle of verbs requires the *-ed* ending. Students should not add *-ed* endings to **infinitives** (*to* + the present form of a verb). Two exercises in correcting errors in verbs complete the discussion.

Verbs called **two-word verbs** contain a verb plus another word, a preposition or adverb. The lesson provides a list of common two-word verbs. Students practice writing sentences with two-word verbs.

A discussion of contractions and verbs completes the lesson. Contractions often contain verbs that ESL students may not recognize in their shortened forms. A practice exercise follows.

Chapter One Test

Place an S above the subject in each sentence and a V above the verb. Place parentheses around each prepositional phrase.

1. The children at the playground were covered with dirt and grass.

2. There is a letter from grandmother in the mailbox.

3. I nearly drowned in the wave pool.

4. Near the bush beside the house is a rabbit with a bushy tail.

5. Barbara and Ted arrived late for dinner at the country club.

6. Where did Philip get the money for the trip?

7. The angry dog barked and growled at the strangers.

8. The tourists traveled to New York for summer vacation.

9. Marie didn't see the child in the street.

10. The meat on the buffet table tastes spicy.

11. My mother and father were not pleased with the new principal.

12. Daria is the president of the club.

13. I do not accept your marriage proposal.

14. Here are the answers to the questions on the test.

15. Jacob decided to drive his van across the desert in California.

16. The cinnamon buns in the bakery smell wonderful.

17. Near the center of town is a statue of a horse.

18. We could have been injured in the car during the storm.

19. Jackson and Diana washed and waxed the car for the customer.

20. I am going to attend college after high school.

Chapter Two Test

I. Combine the sentence pairs using the three options:

   1) a comma and a coordinating conjunction

   2) a semicolon

   3) a semicolon and a conjunctive adverb (with a comma if needed)

The mall closed two hours early.

Michelle did not find a birthday present for her mother.

1. Option 1 _____

2. Option 2 _____

3. Option 3 _____

Bob and his friends spilled drinks and chips on the floor during the game.

The housekeeper refused to clean up the mess.

4. Option 1 _____

5. Option 2 _____

6. Option 3 _____

II. Add a comma, a semicolon, or a semicolon and a conjunctive adverb to the following sentences. Do not add, change, or delete any words.

7. Stephen was not an effective supervisor he was fired last week.

8. Bananas are rich in potassium therefore doctors recommend eating one each day.

9. Will forgot his wife's birthday again and she made him sleep on the couch.

10. Janice placed flowers in each room in the hotel the fresh aroma pleased her guests.

11. Joseph drove his car into the garage then he made sure the doors were locked.

12. The picture on the television was fuzzy so I called a repairman.

13. Barry loved the family camping trips but his wife hated being in the woods.

14. We canceled our reservation as a result we had to forfeit our deposit.

15. The lecture began at eight yet many students did not arrive until nine.

16. Running is a good way to get in shape but it can create several health problems.

17. The vacuum cleaner was on sale however I still could not afford to purchase one.

18. I experienced severe pain in my abdomen so I rushed to the hospital.

19. Baby-sitting toddlers can be a challenging job it requires patience and ingenuity.

20. Bailey lost his new sweater now he has to buy another one.

Chapter Three Test

Correct problems with run-on sentences and comma splices. Some sentences are correct. Label them OK.

1. Jeff rushed through his test, therefore, he made careless mistakes.

2. The band was supposed to practice at noon yet none of the members came to the stadium.

3. Charlie was the best choice for the job he was smart, ambitious, and dedicated.

4. Everyone gathered around the crib to see the baby, but the newborn was fast asleep.

5. The janitors went on strike today they wanted a new vacation policy.

6. I enjoy eating cookies in bed, however, my husband thinks it is a bad habit.

7. We should leave for the airport early, so we do not have to rush to catch our plane.

8. Harry taught his parrot to talk now he can't get it to shut up.

9. Attending summer school can be fun but you have to take it seriously.

10. Martha disliked giving speeches, on the other hand, she did not mind writing them.

11. Jan placed the chicken in the oven and she set the timer for one hour.

12. The twins watch too much television their mother is going to set a time limit.

13. The party ended early so we went home and watched television.

14. The baby-sitter fell asleep on the couch, meanwhile, the kids shaved the dog.

15. Many teens have part-time jobs, but they complain about doing chores at home.

16. The new shoes pinched my toes I could barely walk when the day ended.

17. The burglar stole the antique vase from the mansion so the owner installed a new security
    system.

18. Jessica did not attend the wedding, instead, she came to the reception.

19. Michael panicked when he saw the dog, he darted off the sidewalk and into the oncoming
    traffic.

20. The sheriff searched for the fugitive until sunset, then he organized a search party.

Chapter Four Test

Marcela was afraid of her neighbor's dog.
She never went into the yard alone.

I. Combine the sentences using subordination. Begin the sentences with dependent clauses.

1._____

2._____

The president of the company enforced strict performance standards.
Several of the employees went on strike.

II. Combine the sentences using subordination. End the sentences with dependent clauses.

3._____

4._____

III. Add a comma to each sentence that needs one. Some sentences do not need a comma.

5. Before the park opened the children had to play at home.

6. Michael raced to the mailbox because he expected a letter.

7. The hotel manager will cancel our reservation unless we arrive before noon.

8. Since the dean postponed the lecture the students loitered in the hallway.

9. Whenever the phone rings my poodle barks and growls.

10. I always brush my teeth after meals unless I am away from home.

11. As the teacher raised the flag the students recited the class motto.

12. If the loan officer does not approve my application I will not be able to purchase a house.

13. The judge gave criminals harsh sentences even if their offenses were minor ones.

14. When we arrived at the restaurant the hostess seated us.

15. Jim regretted selling his bike after his car broke down.

44

Chapter Five Test

I. Combine the simple sentences using all five options:
1) a comma and a coordinating conjunction
2) a semicolon
3) a semicolon and a conjunctive adverb (add a comma if needed)
4) using a dependent clause to begin a sentence
5) using a dependent clause to end a sentence

Lisa placed too many clothes in the washing machine.
She didn't bother to read the manufacturer's instructions.

1. _____

2. _____

3. _____

4. _____

5. _____

The clumsy movers dropped the box of dishes.
Shards of glass covered the kitchen floor.

6. _____

7. _____

8. _____

9. _____

10. _____

II. Correct the following sentences adding only commas and semicolons. Do not add,

delete, or capitalize any words.

11. I thought my ankle was broken but I had only sprained it.

12. Joshua refused to cook dinner instead he washed the dishes.

13. Before we painted the room we covered all of the furniture.

14. The baby finally went to sleep he had been crying for hours.

15. Because a fire destroyed the Johnson's house they went to live with relatives.

16. Jerry enjoys outdoors activities therefore he hates rainy days.

17. Maria left her jacket outside it faded in the sun.

18. While the professor was speaking the students listened intently.

19. The lawyer presented damaging evidence however the suspect escaped conviction.

20. Spaghetti is my favorite food so I eat it once a week.

Chapter Six Test

I. Place an S beside each sentence and an F beside each sentences fragment.

___1. Without a chance to be entered in the contest.

___2. Marcy began studying for her college entrance exams during the summer.

___3. The puppy with the brown spots on his back.

___4. For example, college students are often required to perform community service.

___5. Especially the clothes that young girls wear.

___6. Saturday to be the day of the celebration.

___7. After Ben and his wife celebrated their anniversary.

___8. Even though Wanda reduced her work hours, she still did not have time to study.

___9. When the rain ended, the toddlers raced outside.

___10. The students walking to the elementary school.

II. Correct each fragment in the most appropriate way.

11. While waiting for his mother. Jason talked to his best friend.

12. The lady eating by herself.

13. Mary broke up with her boyfriend. And spent the afternoon sulking in her room.

14. John to be announcing his campaign for class president today.

15. The puppy excitedly wagged its tail. As the car pulled into the driveway.

16. Stopping by the side of the road. We watched the horses grazing in the pasture.

17. Communication problems can ruin a relationship. If the couple refuses to get counseling.

18. Whoever delivered the flowers to the wedding chapel.

19. After Marjorie performed in the talent contest. The audience applauded for several minutes.

20. The basketball player standing next to the coach.

Chapter Seven Test

I. Revise the sentences so that they have parallel structure.

1. Good students need to study, attend class, and paying attention is important.

2. We searched for the puppy under the bushes, the backyard, and behind the house.

3. The blouse's color, what it cost, and the light fabric made Amanda want to purchase it.

4. During the summer, we like to swim, bike, and go bowling.

5. Trish is a model with poise, grace, and is beautiful.

6. The party begins at nine; ten is when it ends.

7. The book was interesting, educational, and it had a lot of chapters.

8. After school, I have to pick up my laundry, do my homework, and the dishes have to be washed.

9. I would prefer to swim in the afternoon than watching television.

10. My fiancé is thoughtful, ambitious, and he looks good.

II. Combine each cluster of sentences into one sentence that contains parallel structure.

11. Our new car has comfortable seats.
    It is large enough to hold the entire family.
    The cost did not hurt our budget.

12. The rookie couldn't catch the ball.
    He had problems sliding into home plate.
    He struck out each time he came to bat.

13. Advertisers use humor to sell products.
    Some commercials make viewers cry.
    Some ad agencies resort to scare tactics to sell products.

14. The farmer plowed the field.
    He fed the pigs next.
    He also milked the cows.

15. Marques donates half of his salary to local charities.
    His coworkers consider him a friend.
    During his free times he volunteers at the homeless shelter.

Chapter Eight Test

I. Underline the adjectives in each sentence.

1. A vase of white silk roses was the centerpiece on the table.

2. The largest puppy in the litter looks sleepy.

3. My new red sweater looks good with my white trousers.

4. The oldest child in the family is Chandler.

5. Willie feels sick today.

6. The shy toddler slowly approached the tall man.

7. The beef tacos taste spicy.

8. This curvy road is more dangerous than the highway.

9. Mike works long hours at his new job.

10. The military school is located on a grassy lot.

II. Underline the adverbs in each sentence.

11. The large cat sat gracefully on the windowsill.

12. Sandra quickly returned to her seat.

13. Mark is an extremely bright student.

14. I did well on my English exam.

15. He will speak twice tomorrow.

16. Marcia crossed the narrow bridge slowly and carefully.

17. Yesterday, the judge glanced suspiciously at the lawyer.

18. The roasted almonds were lightly salted.

19. The children performed quite poorly on the practice tests.

20. Joe very carefully groomed his frisky dog.

III. Correct errors in adjective and adverb usage.

21. How good do you know your neighbors?

22. I am more smarter than I was last semester.

23. We felt badly about missing the prom.

24. Mike is taller then his brother Bob.

25. This soda is more sweeter than the lemonade.

26. In court, you need to answer truthful.

27. I live on a long narrow street.

28. My navy, blue dress is in the cleaners.

29. The car passed us quick.

30. Sheila is the most prettiest girl in the pageant.

Chapter Nine Test

I. Some of the following sentences contain misplaced or dangling modifier errors. Correct them by moving, adding, changing, or removing words. Label correct sentences OK.

1. Jake purchased a jacket from the store with a fur collar.

2. After shopping for six hours, the perfect prom dress was purchased.

3. At the age of two, my family moved to New York.

4. The plant is on the table wilted from a lack of water.

5. We purchased bread from the bakery with sesame seeds.

6. Covered with fleas, Monica rescued the stray dog.

7. Rushing to catch the train, a piece of luggage was left behind.

8. Exhausted from working a double shift, the hot shower was quite soothing.

9. Driving through he country, I saw many wild animals.

10. Tripping on the broken sidewalk, I fell nearly to the ground.

11. I found a large snake walking in my backyard.

12. Lost in the woods overnight, the campers were thrilled to see the ranger's cabin.

13. Michelle only wants to have two children.

14. I donated the clothes to the church faded and tattered.

15. Hanging over the fireplace, my guests admired the new painting.

16. Harassed by the school bully, my parents scheduled a meeting with the principal.

17. Fearing a sunburn, the umbrella offered little protection.

18. The cowboy rode his horse wearing chaps and spurs.

19. Tangled in the branches of the tree, we struggled to free the kite.

20. Suspended from the ceiling, the patients could not change the channel on the television.

Chapter Ten Test

Choose the correct verb form in each sentence.

1. Yesterday, Sharon (find/ found) the neighbor's lost kitten.

2. Marcie had (chose/ chosen) her wedding dress months before Don asked her to marry him.

3. Harold (saw/ seen) his best friends leaving the theater.

4. After my dentist filled two cavities in my teeth, I (doesn't/ don't) mind brushing daily.

5. The boxer was (deal/ dealt) a staggering blow in the last round.

6. Only two nurses (was/ were) needed to cover the late shift.

7. It is a crime to (steal/ stole) other's property.

8. The parents (was/ were) impressed by the teacher's commitment to her students.

9. Mary and Tyler (walk/ walks) to their grandmother's house after school.

10. Rosa (feel/ feels) only contempt for her unfaithful husband.

11. I (am/ be) expecting all club members to participate in the rally.

12. The workers (go/ went) on strike after the supervisor reduced their salaries.

13. I (sew/ sewed) three costumes for the school play last fall.

14. After the senator had (spoke/ spoken), a hush fell over the crowd.

15. The pharmacist should have (call/ called) me before he filled the prescription.

16. Each morning, I (do/ does) the breakfast dishes.

17. Johnny's mother often (criticizes/ criticize) his poor performance at work.

18. If the baby (wakes/ wake) up, we won't be able to watch television.

19. The foreigners (has/ have) much to learn about American culture.

20. Wes (was/ were) not sure if the politician was sincere or dishonest.

Chapter Eleven Test

I. Identify the tense of the underlined verb: present, past, present progressive, past progressive, present perfect, or past perfect.

1. I <u>am expecting</u> the package to arrive today.

2. When the birthday party ended, the children <u>had stuffed</u> themselves with cake and ice cream.

3. Jessica <u>braided</u> her hair before leaving for school.

4. By the time Jeff reached home plate, the umpire <u>had stopped</u> the game.

5. Jake <u>was sleeping</u> in his bunk when the platoon sergeant arrived.

6. The actors <u>are practicing</u> their lines for tonight's performance.

7. Mr. Jefferson <u>has been teaching</u> at Lincoln High School for four years.

8. The jury <u>is taking</u> a long time to reach a verdict.

9. Samantha <u>was taking</u> a coffee break when she noticed a rip in her skirt.

10. When the main course arrived, we <u>had finished</u> the appetizer.

11. The carpenter <u>replaced</u> the wooden countertop with a new marble one.

12. The television <u>was blaring</u> in the background when I called home.

13. The reporter <u>looks</u> nervous in front of the camera.

14. I <u>wonder</u> if my colleagues consider me an asset to the company.

15. I <u>have taken</u> this route to work before.

II. Circle the correct form of the verb in each sentence.

16. If the fish (would have/ would of) swam faster, it would not be in the fisherman's net.

17. The soldiers were (supposed to/ suppose to) march in the Veteran's Day Parade.

18. My parents (use to/ used to) attend PTA meetings regularly.

19. I (could of/ could have) passed the test if I had studied more.

20. Sauerkraut (should of/ should have) been served with the sausages.

Chapter Twelve Test

I. Correct inconsistencies in verb tense in the following sentences.

1. We sat in the emergency room for hours before the receptionist calls us.

2. The image on the computer looks distorted, but we ignored it.

3. The restaurant manager apologized for the bad service, offered us discount coupons, and asks us to visit again.

4. Soft music played in the background, yet it annoys the customers.

5. Michael wanted an acoustic guitar for Christmas, but his mother gets him a banjo.

6. No one believes the pearls were real, so we threw them away.

7. When the leaves fall from the trees, we rake them into piles and burned them.

8. Although the wrestler fell on the mat, he is not injured.

9. The maid polished the silver, waxes the floor, and cleaned the shower.

10. The meat loaf was overcooked; it looks burned.

11. I need aspirin for my headache, so I went to the drugstore.

12. Felicia knew the author of the novel, so she asks him to sign her copy.

13. One group of toddlers played in the sandbox; the other group builds houses from blocks.

14. After school, Myra practiced her clarinet, ate a snack, and watches television.

15. The skater slips on the ice and broke his hip.

II. Identify the voice of the following sentences. Change sentences with passive voice to active voice.

16. The unethical governor received a pardon. _____

17. The highway was repaired by the transportation department._____

18. Before his date with Karen, David cleaned the car thoroughly. _____

19. The football fans in the stadium were drenched by the sudden rainstorm. _____

20. The eagle spotted a field mouse hiding in the grass. _____

Chapter Thirteen Test

Circle the correct verb in each sentence.

1. Everybody in the class (is/ are) attending graduation.

2. (Was/ Were) the contestants upset about the cancellation?

3. Sheila and Jan (stay/ stays) at home until their mother arrives.

4. Either Mike or his teammates (was/ were) waiting for the coach.

5. Under my bed with my old shoes (is/ are) a box of clothes.

6. Nobody (expect/ expects) Mike to score a touchdown.

7. They (know/ knows) that fighting is not permitted on the playground.

8. The jury (is/ are) arguing amongst themselves about the case.

9. Neither of the boys (has/ have) enough money to buy lunch.

10. Where (was/ were) the cat and dog sleeping before you purchased the cages?

11. The rooster or the chickens (was/ were) eating the grain left in the pail.

12. Neither Ted nor his sisters (want/ wants) to move to Kansas.

13. The clowns with the large hats (is/ are) quite amusing to the children.

14. Here (is/ are) a pad and a pen to take notes with in class.

15. All members of the team (is/ are) practicing for the championship game.

16. Anybody with a small child (know/ knows) the importance of patience.

17. The audience (is/ are) demanding a refund because of the actor's poor performance.

18. There (is/ are) several questions on the census form.

19. Near the center of town (is/ are) a statue of the town's founder.

20. Not only my son but also my daughter (was/ were) planning to visit me during spring break.

Chapter Fourteen Test

I. Choose the correct pronoun in each sentence.

1. Sales have increased, so everybody (is/ are) expecting a large bonus.

2. Several prominent men (is/ are) speaking at the presidential rally.

3. The jury had to remain in (its/ their) chamber until the courtroom was empty.

4. Someone in the drama club (has/ have) to be responsible for stage decoration.

5. This week the class (is/ are) learning multiplication.

6. Neither of the girls can explain why (she/ they) is late for class.

7. We applaud loudly even when our team (is/ are) losing the game.

8. Mike and Jason are vacationing in Florida; (he/ they) will not return until Saturday.

9. The members of the council decided to rewrite (its/ their) bylaws.

10. Everyone must strive to do (his/ their) best at work.

II. Rewrite the following sentences so that the pronouns have clear reference. You can add, take out, or change words.

11. The librarian took the books from the boxes and gave them to her assistant.

12. Mary had to take a bus to her job which she detested.

13. Brad told his manager that he needed to take a vacation.

14. When there are several customers in the store, they open another check-out lane.

15. The legislator gave a speech on tax hikes which angered his constituents.

16. Jessica always takes her car to Quick Fix for repairs because they have the lowest rates in town.

17. Martha gave Sue a present when she left for college.

18. When Paula bumped her head on the table it hurt.

19. Michelle arrived at the auditorium two hours before the show, but he said all the tickets were sold.

20. Take the cake out of the pan, and put it on the table.

Chapter Fifteen Test

I. Correct errors in consistency of pronouns.

1. Retailers will get more customers if you keep prices low.

2. I clean my house on Saturday because you don't have time during the week.

3. We were not pleased with the new attendance policy since you still had to receive permission to miss a class.

4. I enjoy hiking in the mountains because you can see the distant villages.

5. The tourists stayed on the beach because you couldn't swim in shark-infested water.

6. We did not park in the hotel's lot because you had to pay a fee.

7. Toddlers need an afternoon nap; you are tired from the morning's activities.

8. Shoppers know the store is about to close when you see the clerks counting the money.

9. I try to avoid rush-hour traffic; you have to leave home an hour early.

10. We eat dinner at McDuff's frequently; you never have to wait for a table.

II. Choose the correct pronoun in each sentence.

11. The singer gave a special performance for Lou and (she/ her).

12. Between you and (I/ me), I don't think Joan is qualified for the management position.

13. My best friends and (I/ me) didn't want to attend different colleges after graduation.

14. The movie was boring to Jessica and (I/ me).

15. The teacher and (I/ me) stayed after class to review the assignment.

16. The shampoo is designed to give bounce and body to (you/ your) hair.

17. The photographer sent Ted and (she/ her) a bill for the portraits.

18. The volunteers and (he/ him) tutored at the youth center after school.

19. It was hard for (we/ us) to remain patient after hours of waiting.

20. The family donated (its/ it's) family heirlooms to the museum.

21. Samantha gave Ted and (she/ her) a ride to work.

22. (He/ Him) and (she/ her) called a taxi when the car wouldn't start.

23. The party was a surprise for my mother and (myself/ me).

24. The mechanic and (us/ she) argued about the cost of the repairs.

25. Mom divided the money between Jeff and (I/ me).

Chapter Sixteen Test

In the following sentences, correct any punctuation errors. Add punctuation where it is needed.

1. I chose Great Expectations for my book report but I didnt read it.

2. The meeting didnt end at six pm it ended at ten pm.

3. Mike purchased the supplies for the trip flashlights batteries matches and tents.

4. Unfortunately the promoters canceled the concert because of rain.

5. Debra wore a lime green blazer to the costume party.

6. Joseph and I were married on September 2 1988 in Montgomery AL.

7. I plan to visit spain in the fall therefore I need to get a passport.

8. In my literature class we read a short story called The New Breed.

9. My boyfriend eats pork rinds which I hate every night.

10. The split level house on Elm St. belongs to Dr Michaels.

11. janet jackson sang Control at madison square garden.

12. The new refrigerator costs seven hundred and fifty dollars.

13. Whatever you say say it correctly.

14. Dr. Kelly teaches english 121 at oakland university.

15. Ryan's Bistro the oldest restaurant in town collapsed during the earthquake.

16. Young students often forget to dot their *i*s and cross their *t*s.

17. A snake is wrapped around your leg

18. We spoke to college recruiters from Charlotte North Carolina Phoenix Arizona Boston Massachusetts and Springfield Illinois.

19. My family moved to georgia because winters in the south are mild.

20. Gizelle asked Does father go to work on tuesday

21. Jeffs father couldnt afford a new car so Jeff had to walk to high school.

22. Before I moved to Oakland Cal. I lived in the east.

23. It took a months salary to pay for Elizabeths custom made engagement ring.

24. Take some tylenol for your headache said mr Jones.

25. Wendy ripped her dress she smudged her makeup and she refused to go to the prom.

Chapter Seventeen Test

I. Combine the following words and endings.

1. dainty + ness

2. defense + ive

3. move + able

4. inspect + ing

5. pen + ed

6. ounce + es

7. study + ed

8. grave + ly

9. pitch = es

10. motivate + ed

II. Apply the rules for using *ie* or *ei* in the following sentences.

11. f _ _ ry

12. b _ _ ge

13. dec _ _ t

14. gr _ _ ve

15. v _ _ l

III. Circle the correct word in parentheses in each sentence.

16. A fire (can not/ cannot) continue to burn without oxygen.

17. We dashed into a (nearby/ near by) building to use the (bathroom/ bath room).

18. The master (bedroom/ bed room) is located (downstairs/ down stairs).

19. I do not live on Elm Street (any more/ anymore).

20. (Everyone/ Every one) of my classmates graduated from the local (high school/ highschool).

21. We advertised for a (room mate/ roommate) to share the apartment.

22. Most parents spend (alot/ a lot) of time helping their children with homework.

23. Martha said (good-bye/ good by) to her date when they reached the porch.

24. My (grandmother/ grand mother) worked as a (schoolteacher/ school teacher) for thirty

    years before she retired.

25. By the time the second shift arrived, the nurses had (all ready/ already) medicated the

    patients.

Chapter Eighteen Test

Select the correct word in the parentheses.

1. The next (edition/ addition) of the newspaper has an article about the school's new (principal/ principle).

2. The pilot of the (plain/ plane) began his (descent/ decent) to the airport.

3. The city (counsel/ council) has scheduled a meeting to discuss (it's / its) new agenda.

4. All of the (personnel/ personal) at the factory (past/ passed) the health examination.

5. The groom stood (beside/ besides) his bride at the (altar/ alter).

6. The soldiers (knew/ new) that the rendezvous area was (farther/ further) down the road.

7. Bob is (to/ too/ two) tired (to/ too/ two) work for (to/ too/ two) more hours.

8. Mary tried in (vain/ vane/ vein) to get the tight jeans fastened at her (waste/ waist).

9. The twins found (there/ they're/ their) Christmas (presence/ presents) under the tree.

10. (Your/ You're) going to (loose/ lose) the chess title if you don't practice.

11. Visitors need to be (quite/ quiet) when they visit (patience/ patients) at the hospital.

12. We must (choose/ chose) the (cloths/ clothes) that we will (buy/ by) for the trip.

13. This is the (fourth/ forth) time that we served (steak/ stake) in the cafeteria this month.

14. The (flower/ flour) grew even though there was no (rein/ reign/ rain) in the (desert/ dessert).

15. The wind has an (effect/ affect) on the operation of the weather (vein/ vane/ vain).

16. No one is (allowed/ aloud) to drive (threw/ through) town because the road is flooded.

17. The lioness chose (a/ an/ and) (sight/ site/ cite) where she could safely deliver her cubs.

18. Marcy (would/ wood) rather go home (than/ then) stay here.

19. The (angle/ angel) will (brake/ break) if it falls from the top of the tree.

20. Mac's (conscious/ conscience) bothered him after he stole a (peace/ piece) of (you're/ your) furniture.

Chapter Nineteen Test

Circle the correct preposition in each of the following sentences.

1. The umbrella will protect your clothes (from/ against) the rain.

2. I will meet you (on/ at) the corner of Crenshaw and Main.

3. Try to arrive (to/ at) my house before the guests.

4. The Democrat differs (from/ with) the Republican on the tax issue.

5. The club officers are responsible (for/ to) the faculty advisors.

6. Sharon and I decided to divide the money (among/ between) us.

7. I am grateful (to/ for) the foundation for my scholarship.

8. At the restaurant, his job is to wait (for/ on) the customers.

9. The science teacher did not succeed (in/ at) his efforts to acquire a grant.

10. The teenager missed his curfew and tried to reason (for/ with) his parents.

11. Most swimmers prefer the pool (to/ over) the ocean.

12. Kelly is popular (with/ to) his classmates.

13. The manager will call (to/ on) Marion to run the new store.

14. The employee became acquainted (with/ to) the other workers.

15. The newest model of the car is superior (to/ from) the prototype.

16. The morning classes are convenient (to/ for) teachers with young children.

17. The CEO uses memos to correspond (to/ with) the employees in the firm.

18. Mom relied (on/ to) her instincts when she was unsure.

19. The secretary is responsible (for/ to) making copies of the rosters.

20. Jason's ideas are often similar (with/ to) mine.

Chapter Twenty Test

I. Some of the items on the list are topics; label them T. Some are too broad to be developed in a paragraph; label them B. Some are too narrow to be developed in a paragraph; label them N. Some items are announcements; label them A. Label good topic sentences TS.

_____ 1. An easy way to make money.

_____ 2. This paragraph is about basketball.

_____ 3. Crime in America has increased in the last century.

_____ 4. Going to night school has three advantages.

_____ 5. Mike loaned me his hammer.

_____ 6. Sports are a favorite pastime in many countries.

_____ 7. Drinking and driving will be discussed in my paper.

_____ 8. My part-time job taught me the meaning of responsibility.

_____ 9. Our new baby is a boy.

_____10. How to cut hair.

II. Write an appropriate topic sentence for each list of details.

11. Topic sentence

_____

_____

We have to get up for two and four a.m. feedings.
Baby furniture replaced the den furniture.
We use movie money for diapers.
Most of our conversations are about the baby.

12. Topic sentence

_____

_____

Jake plays soccer each weekend.
He never misses any neighborhood soccer matches.
He spends several hours on the internet each day getting soccer scores.

His wallpaper has soccer players on it.

13. Topic sentence

_____

_____

I spent most of my summer wages on movies.
I treated my friends to pizza each week.
I didn't buy any clothes or school supplies.
My mother refused to buy my school supplies.
I was embarrassed when I had to borrow paper and pencils from my classmates.

14. Topic sentence

_____

_____

I don't understand math terminology.
I can't operate my calculator.
I failed half of the tests.
My math tutor could not help me understand the material.

15. Topic sentence

_____

_____

It is easier to get a parking space at the college at night than during the daytime.
The sizes of night classes are smaller than day classes.
There is more time at night for teacher-student interaction than during the day.
The library and computer lab are not crowded at night.
Students can earn money at higher-paying day jobs and still attend college.

Chapter Twenty-One Test

I. Add three details to support each topic sentence.

In the afternoon, I avoid the gym for a number of reasons.

1. _____

2. _____

3. _____

Owning a car can be a financial drain.

4. _____

5. _____

6. _____

II. Cross out details that do not relate to the topic sentence.

7. Topic sentence: My husband takes me for granted.

   He never compliments my cooking; he only points out shortcomings.

   He leaves dirty clothes on the floor for me to pick up.

   His mother treats him like a little boy.

   When his relatives visit, he expects me to cook and clean for them.

   Last year, my friend divorced her husband.

8. Topic sentence: Maria is an ideal nurse.

   She often remains after her shift is over to help the other nurses.

   She graduated from Jackson University.

   She never gets angry with rude patients.

   She spends several hours each week in classes to improve her nursing skills.

   After Maria received the Nursing Excellence Award, Barbara was jealous.

III. Put the details in the correct order.

9. Topic sentence: Jackie prepared her poodle for the dog show. (Put the sentences in space order, from head to tail)

_____ She carefully cleaned his teeth.

_____ She trimmed the fur on its tail into two round puffs.

_____ She made sure the excess fur on his belly was removed.

_____ Next, she brushed the fur on its back.

10. Topic sentence: Smoking can have several negative effects. (Put the sentences in emphatic order, from the least important effect to the most important)

_____ Secondary smoke can be harmful to other people.

_____ The escalating prices of cigarettes prevents some smokers from buying necessities.

_____ The smell of smoke lingers in the clothes of the smokers.

_____ Smoking often results in lung cancer and other respiratory ailments.

Chapter Twenty-Two Test

I. Revise the paragraph for unity. Cross out the sentences that do not fit the topic sentence. The topic sentence is the first sentence in the paragraph.

Toddlers often learn negative behavior from their playmates. Young children acquire most of their social skills through interaction with other children their age. When I was little, I only played with children at the daycare center. Unfortunately, they sometimes adopt undesirable behavioral patterns such as throwing tantrums when they are displeased. If a child witnesses such behavior, the youngster may imitate the act at home, hoping for a similar outcome. Sometimes adults throw tantrums. Another negative trait that is often mimicked is fighting. A child who is bullied or sees aggressive behavior may resort to fighting to resolve disputes as well. Parents must make their impressionable toddlers understand what does and does not constitute acceptable behavior.

II. Revise the paragraph for unity. One sentence is in the wrong place. Move it to the right place by drawing an arrow from the sentence to its proper place.

Marielle anxiously awaited the first day of school. She was halfway to the bus stop before she realized that it was Sunday. She woke up early and rushed to the bathroom before her brother beat her to it. She stayed in front of the mirror longer than usual, checking and rechecking her hair, makeup, and clothes. She wanted her appearance to be flawless. Marielle ate her breakfast without tasting it and dashed out of the house.

III. Revise the paragraph for style. The paragraph is repetitive in its word choice. Replace each underlined word with one that is less repetitive. Write the new word above the underlined one.

William's new job does not allow him to spend much time with his family. He works hard and is very tired when he gets home. He is too <u>tired</u> to give his daughters a horsy ride. His <u>daughters</u> complain when he doesn't play with them. William's wife wants him to discuss the day's events, but he always falls asleep while she <u>discusses</u> her day. He only wants to crawl into his comfortable bed. After a <u>hard</u> day at work, William prefers his <u>comfortable</u> bed, not family activities.

IV. Revise the paragraph to correct run-on sentences and sentence fragments.

Taking care of Peanut, our miniature dachshund, made my family realize that small pets require more attention than large ones. Peanut cannot be left alone outside he can squeeze through small openings in the fence and run into the street. Peanut can also get into small spaces inside the house. Such as under the bookcase and behind the dryer. Peanut's favorite pastime is chewing things he gnaws on shoes, toys, books, and furniture. Everything except his chew toys. Even though we must constantly watch Peanut, we love him and can't imagine our lives without him.

Chapter Twenty-Three Test

Proofread the following paragraph for errors in word choice, spelling, punctuation, and mechanics. Correct the fifteen errors by crossing out each mistake and writing the correction above it.

Commuting to her new job created several problem for Kelly. She had to get out of bed at six am in order too arive at work on time. Kelly was often very sleepy as she showered and dressed. Sense she left here house so early, kelly could know longer eat breakfast with her daughters. they were steal asleep when she began her day. Another problem was traffic. Kelly was often delayed bye traffic acidents, school busses, and slow driver's. When her workday finally ended, she had to make the long drive back home. By the time she arrived, she was exhausted. The next time she excepted a job, it would be in the town where she lived.

Chapter Twenty-Four Test

I. For the topic sentences and lists of details, decide which order would be most appropriate for organizing the list: time order, space order, or emphatic order.

1. Topic sentence: Juan used great skill to sculpt a life-size statue for the museum.

   He carved long, flowing locks of hair for the head.
   A loincloth covered the midsection.
   Its powerful arms were extended above its head.
   The figure was barefooted.
   The stone legs rippled with muscles.

   _____

2. Topic sentence: Margaret carefully planned her wedding reception.

   She purchased the invitations.
   She selected the music.
   She made a list of guests to invite.
   She met with the caterer to plan the menu.
   She decided to decorate the hall with candles instead of flowers.

   _____

3. Topic sentence: Carla had to leave college for several reasons.

   She didn't like her professors.
   She stayed up too late at night and often overslept.
   She needed to work full time to pay her bills.
   She was doing poorly in her classes.
   Her father refused to pay her tuition because she was behaving irresponsibly.

   _____

II. Write a topic sentence for each list of details.

4. Topic sentence

   _____

   _____

I worked all summer at the computer lab to save money for my apartment.
I use my earnings to pay for expenses such as rent, utilities, and food.
I no longer waste money on clothes and movies.
Since my mother is no longer available, I cook my own meals and do my own laundry.
I have to make sure that I get up in time to get to work.

5. Topic sentence

_____

_____

Cats adapt quickly to using the litter box.
Cats groom themselves frequently.
Owners can leave cats alone for several hours.
Cats are very affectionate.
Compared to dogs, cats are quiet animals.

III. In each outline, cross out details that do not relate to the topic sentence.

6. Topic sentence: My daughters do not get along well.

Daria likes to break Dee's toys.
Dee teases Daria and makes her cry.
Dee is older than Daria.
At dinner time, they throw food at each other.
They call each other names like "Fathead" and "Dummy."
Many brothers and sisters argue.

7. Topic sentence: Jeff is an ideal father.

He helps the children with homework after dinner.
He takes his children to sporting events, movies, and concerts.
He works as an architect.
He reads the children bedtime stories each night.
His best friend does not have any children.
Each day he hugs his children and tells them he loves them.

IV. Each of the following outlines has one detail that is out of order. Indicate where it belongs by drawing an arrow from it to the place where it should go.

8. Topic sentence: Debbie's poor dental hygiene caused her many problems.

Debbie forget to brush her teeth after meals.
She didn't floss her teeth because she was too busy.
She had to schedule a dental appointment.
Her teeth began to hurt.
The dentist said that she had ten cavities.
Some of her teeth had to be removed.
Debbie had to pay hundreds of dollars to have her cavities filled.

9. Topic sentence: Drinking and driving can be quite dangerous.

Drunk drivers often think that they are sober enough to drive.
Drunk drivers are not alert to conditions around them.
Thousands of people die each year because of drunk drivers.
They ignore stop signs and traffic lights.
Drunk drivers are responsible for one-third of all traffic accidents.

V. Put the details in the outline in the correct order.

10. Topic sentence: Getting my new dog home from the pound was a challenge.

_____ Rex urinated in the back seat of my car and chewed on the upholstery.

_____ My neighbors helped me catch him and bring him back inside.

_____ It took two workers at the pound to get Rex out of his cage.

_____ He barked and growled as I led him out to my car.

_____ As soon as I put him down, he ran out the front door and into the yard.

_____ When we arrived at my house, he wouldn't move, so I had to carry him inside.

Chapter Twenty-Five Test

I. Replace the underlined word in each sentence with a more specific word.

1. The spaghetti was <u>great</u>.

2. Your new shirt looks <u>bad.</u>

3. I paid a <u>bundle</u> for my new house.

4. This milk smells <u>funny</u>.

5. This is a <u>good</u> book.

II. List four specific words or clauses for each general term.

6. bread:

7. pet:

8. relative:

9. tree:

10. sport:

III. Add two details for each outline.

11. Topic sentence: I prefer being married to being single.

    Raising children is easier when the parents are married.

    I do not have to worry about getting a date.

    _____

    _____

12. Topic sentence: Running is an excellent form of exercise.

    It can be done indoors and outdoors.

    There is no expensive equipment to buy.

    _____

    _____

IV. Write sense words for the following items.

13. Write two sense words or phrases to describe the taste of a lemon.

14. Write two sense words or phrases to describe the sounds of a disco.

15. Write two sense words or phrases to describe the texture of a blanket.

Chapter Twenty-Six Test

I. List the three steps of the writing from reading process.

1.

2.

3.

II. What does "attitude" refer to in regards to the reading process?

4.

III. List four of the items that should be considered during the first step of the reading process.

5.

6.

7.

8.

IV. List four actions that are performed during the last phase of the reading process.

9.

10.

11.

12.

V. List three things that must be included in a summary of a reading.

13.

14.

15.

Appendix Test

I. Label the nouns as count or noncount.

1. table

2. sand

3. sandwich

4. book

5. furniture

6. water

7. experience

8. student

9. cookie

10. dedication

II. Insert *a*, *an*, or *the* in the blanks.

11. I was ___ first child in my family to buy ___ car.

12. My house is ___ one with ___ awning over the door.

13. My dog ate most of ___ food I bought.

14. Maria made ___ food for ___ friend.

15. ___ babies slept through ___ night.

III. Correct errors in subjects.

16. When returns home, Janet will go to bed.

17. Mr. Jones he never works at night.

18. I like to visit the zoo; love to look at the animals.

19. Went to the library yesterday.

20. The students study because want to do well in class.

IV. Correct errors in verbs in the sentences.

21. The sick child look pale.

22. Amy was happy because she had finish her exams.

23. Yesterday, I walk to the library to study.

24. Meat necessary for a healthy diet.

25. He read and write well for his age.

V. Write a sentence for each two-word verb.

26. run into:

27. fill in:

28. keep on:

29. ask out:

30. drop in:

VI. Write out each contraction in its long form.

31. I don't want to eat spinach.

32. They'll be at the restaurant when you arrive.

33. I'm sure I mailed the letter.

34. Let's go to the museum later.

35. It's too hot to play outside.

ANSWER KEY TO CHAPTER TESTS

Chapter One Test

1. S-children V-were covered
   at the playground
   with dirt and grass
2. S-letter V-is
   from grandmother
   in the mailbox
3. S-I   V-drowned
   in the wave pool
4. S-rabbit   V-is
   Near the bush
   beside the house
   with a bushy tail
5. S-Barbara, Ted   V-arrived
   for dinner
   at the country club
6. S-Philip V-did get
   for the trip
7. S-dog   V-barked, growled
   at the strangers
8. S-tourists V-traveled
   to New York
   for summer vacation
9. S-Marie V-did see
   in the street
10. S-meat V-tastes
    on the buffet table
11. S-mother, father V-were pleased
    with the new principal
12. S-Daria V-is
    of the club
13. S-I V-do accept
14. S-answers V-are
    to the questions
    on the test
15. S-Jacob V-decided
    across the desert
    in California
16. S-buns V-smell
    in the bakery
17. S-statue V-is
    Near the center
    of town

of a horse
18. S-We V-could have been injured
    in the car
    during the storm
19. S-Jackson, Diana V-washed, waxed
    for the customer
20. S-I V-am going
    after high school

Chapter Two Test

1, 3, 4, 6 Answers vary
2. The mall closed two hours early; Michelle did not find a birthday present for her mother.
5. Bob and his friends spilled drinks and chips on the floor during the game; the housekeeper refused to clean up the mess.
7. supervisor; he
8. potassium; therefore,
9. again, and
10. hotel; the
11. garage; then
12. fuzzy, so
13. trips, but
14. reservation; as a result,
15. eight, yet
16. shape, but
17. sale; however,
18. abdomen, so
19. job; it
20. sweater; now

Chapter Three Test

1. test; therefore,
2. noon, yet
3. job; he
4. OK
5. today; they
6. bed; however,
7. OK
8. talk; now
9. fun, but
10. speeches; on the other hand,
11. oven, and
12. television; their
13. early, so
14. couch; meanwhile,

15. OK
16. toes; I
17. mansion, so
18. wedding; instead,
19. dog; he
20. sunset; then

Chapter Four Test
1-4 Answers vary
5. opened, the
6. OK
7. OK
8. canceled, the
9. rings, my
10. OK
11. raised, the
12. application, I
13. OK
14. restaurant, the
15. OK

Chapter Five Test
1-10 Answers vary
11. broken, but
12. dinner; instead,
13. room, we
14. sleep; he
15. house, they
16. activities; therefore,
17. outside; it
18. speaking, the
19. evidence; however,
20. food, so

Chapter Six Test
1. F
2. S
3. F
4. S
5. F
6. F
7. F
8. S
9. S

10. F
11-20 Answers vary

Chapter Seven Test
Answers vary

Chapter Eight Test
1. white, silk
2. largest, sleepy
3. new, red, good, white
4. oldest
5. sick
6. shy, tall
7. beef, spicy
8. curvy, dangerous
9. long, new
10. military, grassy
11. gracefully
12. quickly
13. extremely
14. well
15. twice, tomorrow
16. slowly, carefully
17. Yesterday, suspiciously
18. lightly
19. quite, poorly
20. very, carefully
21. How well do you know your neighbors?
22. I am smarter than I was last semester.
23. We felt bad about missing the prom.
24. Mike is taller than his brother Bob.
25. This soda is sweeter than the lemonade.
26. In court, you need to answer truthfully.
27. I live on a long, narrow street.
28. My navy blue dress is in the cleaners.
29. The car passed us quickly.
30. Sheila is the prettiest girl in the pageant.

Chapter Nine Test
9. OK
12. OK
1-8, 10-11, 13-20 Answers Vary--Possible answers:
1. Jake purchased a jacket with a fur collar from the store.
2. After Mary shopped for six hours, she purchased the perfect prom dress.

3. When I was two, my family moved to New York.
4. Wilted from a lack of water, the plant is on the table.
5. We purchased bread with sesame seeds from the bakery.
6. Monica rescued the stray dog covered with fleas.
7. When we were rushing to catch the train, a piece of luggage was left behind.
8. Because Jack was exhausted from working a double shift, the hot shower was quite soothing.
9. OK
10. Tripping on the sidewalk, I nearly fell to the ground.
11. Walking in my backyard, I found a large snake.
12. OK
13. Michelle wants to have only two children.
14. I donated faded and tattered clothes to the church.
15. My guests admired the new painting hanging over the fireplace.
16. After the school bully harassed me, my parents scheduled a meeting with the principal.
17. The umbrella offered little protection to the lady fearing a sunburn.
18. Wearing chaps and spurs, the cowboy rode his horse.
19. We struggled to free the kite tangled in the branches of the tree.
20. The patients could not change the channel on the television suspended from the ceiling.

Chapter Ten Test
1. found
2. chosen
3. saw
4. don't
5. dealt
6. were
7. steal
8. were
9. walk
10. feels
11. am
12. went
13. sewed
14. spoken
15. called
16. do
17. criticizes
18. wakes
19. have
20. was

Chapter Eleven Test
1. present progressive
2. past perfect

3. past
4. past perfect
5. past progressive
6. present progressive
7. present perfect
8. present progressive
9. past progressive
10. past perfect
11. past
12. past progressive
13. present
14. present
15. present perfect
16. had
17. supposed to
18. used to
19. could have
20. should have

Chapter Twelve Test

1-15 **Answers Vary**
16, 17, 19--Part 2 of answer varies.
16. Passive
   The president gave the unethical governor a pardon.
17. Passive
   The transportation department repaved the highway.
18. Active
19. Passive
   The sudden rainstorm drenched the football fans in the stadium.
20. Active

Chapter Thirteen Test

1. is
2. Were
3. stay
4. were
5. is
6. expects
7. know
8. are
9. has
10. were
11. were

12. were
13. want
14. are
15. are
16. knows
17. is
18. are
19. is
20. was

Chapter Fourteen Test
1. is
2. are
3. its
4. has
5. is
6. she
7. is
8. they
9. their
10. his
11-20 Answers vary

Chapter Fifteen Test
1-10 Answers vary
11. her
12. me
13. I
14. him
15. I
16. your
17. me
18. he
19. us
20. its
21. her
22. He, she
23. me
24. we
25. me

Chapter Sixteen Test
1. I chose <u>Great Expectations</u> for my book report, but I didn't read it.
2. The meeting didn't end at six p.m.; it ended at ten p.m..

3. Mike purchased the supplies for the trip: flashlights, batteries, matches, and tents.
4. Unfortunately, the promoters canceled the concert because of rain.
5. Debra wore a lime-green blazer to the costume party.
6. Joseph and I were married on September 2, 1988, in Montgomery, Alabama.
7. I plan to visit Spain in the fall; therefore, I need to get a passport.
8. In my literature class, we read a short story called "The New Breed."
9. My boyfriend eats pork rinds-which I hate- every night. (Commas or parentheses may be used)
10. The split-level house on Elm Street belongs to Dr. Michaels.
11. Janet Jackson sang "Control" at Madison Square Garden.
12. The new refrigerator costs $750.
13. Whatever you say, say it correctly.
14. Dr. Kelly teaches English 121 at Oakland University.
15. Ryan's Bistro, the oldest restaurant in town, collapsed during the earthquake. (Dashes or parentheses may be used)
16. Young students often forget to dot their *i*'s and cross their *t*'s.
17. A snake is wrapped around your leg!
18. We spoke to college recruiters from Charlotte, North Carolina; Phoenix, Arizona; Boston, Massachusetts; and Springfield, Illinois.
19. My family moved to Georgia because winters in the South are mild.
20. Gizelle asked, "Does Father go to work on Tuesday?"
21. Jeff's father couldn't afford a new car, so Jeff had to walk to the high school.
22. Before I moved to Oakland, California, I lived in the East.
23. It took a month's salary to pay for Elizabeth's custom-made engagement ring.
24. "Take some Tylenol for your headache," said Mr. Jones.
25. Wendy ripped her dress, she smudged her makeup, and she refused to go to the prom.

Chapter Seventeen Test
1. daintiness
2. defensive
3. moveable
4. inspecting
5. penned
6. ounces
7. studied
8. gravely
9. pitches
10. motivated
11. fiery
12. beige
13. deceit
14. grieve
15. veil
16. cannot

17. nearby. bathroom
18. bedroom, downstairs
19. anymore
20. Every one
21. roommates
22. a lot
23. good-bye
24. grandmother, schoolteacher
25. already

Chapter Eighteen Test
1. edition, principal
2. plane, descent
3. council, its
4. personnel, passed
5. beside, altar
6. knew, farther
7. too, to, two
8. vain, waist
9. their, presents
10. You're lose
11. quiet, patients
12. chose, clothes, buy
13. fourth, steak
14. flower, rain, desert
15. effect, vane
16. allowed, through
17. a, site
18. would, than
19. angel, break
20. conscience, piece, your

Chapter Nineteen Test
1. against
2. at
3. at
4. with
5. to
6. between
7. to
8. on
9. in
10. with
11. to

12. with
13. on
14. with
15. to
16. for
17. with
18. on
19. for
20. to

Chapter Twenty Test

1. T
2. A
3. B
4. TS
5. N
6. B
7. A
8. TS
9. N
10. T
11-15 Answers vary

Chapter Twenty-One Test

1-6 Answers vary
7. His mother treats him like a little boy.
    Last year, my friend Linda divorced her husband.
8. She graduated from Jackson University
    After Maria received the Nursing Excellence Award, Barbara was jealous.
9. 1, 4, 3, 2
10. 3, 2, 1, 4

Chapter Twenty-Two Test

I. When I was little I only played with children at the daycare center.
   Sometimes adults throw tantrums.
II. She was halfway to the bus stop before she realized it was Sunday. (This should be the last sentence in the paragraph.
III and IV Answers vary

Chapter Twenty-Three Test

   Commuting to her new job created several problems for Kelly. She had to get out of bed at six a.m. in order to arrive at work on time. Kelly was often very sleepy as she showered and dressed. Since she left her house so early, Kelly could no longer eat breakfast with her daughters. They were still asleep when she began her day. Another problem was traffic. Kelly was often delayed <u>by</u> traffic <u>accidents</u>, school <u>buses</u>, and slow <u>drivers</u>. When her work day finally ended, she had to make the long drive back home. By the time she arrived, she was exhausted. The next time she <u>accepted</u> a job, it would be in the town where she lived.

Chapter Twenty-Four Test

1. space
2. time
3. emphatic
4-5 Answers vary
6. Dee is older than Daria.
   Many brothers and sisters fight.
7. He works as an architect.
   His best friend does not have any kids.
8. Her teeth began to hurt. (This should be the third sentence in the outline)
9. Thousands of people die each year because of drunk drivers. (This should be the last sentence in the outline)
10. 3, 6, 1, 2. 5. 4

Chapter Twenty-Five Test

Answers vary

Chapter Twenty-Six Test

1-3 Order may vary
1. preread
2. read
3. reread with a pen or pencil
4. Thinking of what is read as half of a conversation
5-8 length, subheadings, charts, graphs, photographs or illustrations, introductory materials or introductory questions, background on the author or subject, boxed or highlighted material, title
9-12 mark main point, mark other points, define words, ask questions, evaluate the writer's ideas, react to the writer's opinions or examples, add ideas, opinions. or examples
13-15 Order may very
13. the writer's main idea
14. the ideas used to explain the main idea   } Order may vary
15. some examples or details

Appendix Test

1. C
2. N
3. C
4. C
5. N
6. N

7. N
8. C
9. C
10. N
11. the, a
12. the, an
13. the
14. the, a
15. The, the
16. When she returns home, Janet will go to bed.
17. Mr. Jones never works at night.
18. I like to visit the zoo; I love to look at the animals.
19. Answer varies
20. The students study because they want to do well in class.
21. The sick child looks pale.
22. Amy was happy because she had finished her exams.
23. Yesterday, I walked to the library to study.
24. Meat is necessary for a healthy diet.
25. He reads and writes well for his age.
26-30 Answers vary
31. do not
32. They will
33. I am
34. Let us
35. It is

Summaries of Reading Selections

"Binge Nights: The Emergency on Campus" Michael Winerip

A college student learns the consequences of binge drinking when it nearly costs him his life. After passing out at a football game, he awakens in the intensive care unit of the hospital and vows never to drink again.

"The Baby Myna" Ved Mehta

Caring for a pet myna proves to be a challenge for its blind owner. When the bird learns to speak, its value to its owner is enhanced. The boy realizes the power of instinct when he, against his instinct, allows the bird to venture outside the cage, and the bird follows instinct and secures its freedom.

"I Fell in Love, Or My Hormones Awakened" Judith Ortiz Cofer

A young Puerto Rican girl becomes infatuated with an older student. She learns that "adulation leaves a scent" when the object of her attraction delivers her first kiss, sending her hormones into overdrive.

"I Wish" Lillian Gwin

A Native-American girl longs for a return to the world of her ancestors. Although she must accept the world created by whites, she does not lose hope for change in the future.

"Death Row" John Grisham

A death-row inmate enjoys a thunderstorm the prisoners' only relief from the stifling heat of the Mississippi prison. Listening to the rain, he imagines a naked romp on the prison grounds.

"A Different Mirror" Ronald Takaki

Signs of America's ethnic diversity appear in the names of cities, the language, the music, and the occupations.

"Part-Time Jobs May Do Teenagers More Harm Than Good" Gary Holt

Many teenagers choose part-time jobs to purchase instant-gratification items. Parents support these efforts, feeling their children will learn responsibility and useful job skills. However, studies prove that students who work long hours perform poorly in school, miss extracurricular activities, and display behavioral problems.

"New Directions" Maya Angelou

Annie Johnson demonstrates her survival instincts when she must support herself and her children after her husband abandons them. Relying on her skills as a cook, she begins a business selling meat pies to the factory workers. The small enterprise develops into a country store.

"Home Away From Home" Beth Nieman

A home day-care provider discusses the role she plays in the lives of children and their parents. She explains the consequences of parents missing payments and bringing sick children to the center. Though she is more often criticized than complimented, Nieman enjoys her job, especially since she can care for her own children.

Sample Sixteen-Week Syllabus
(Adaptable for eight or twelve-week courses)

The sixteen-week format can be adjusted for flexible scheduling:

* For an eight-week "express term," double the assignments.

*For twelve-week terms, sections of Chapters 24-26 may be incorporated into the discussions of Chapters 20-23.

Week One
Class overview
Chapter One (The Simple Sentence)
Test Chapter One

Week Two
Chapter 2 (Coordination) and Chapter 3 (Avoiding Run-on Sentences and Comma Splices)

Week Three
Test Chapters 2 and 3
Chapter 4 (Subordination) and Chapter 5 (Combining Sentences: A Review)

Week Four
Test Chapters 4 and 5
Chapter 6 (Avoiding Sentence Fragments) and Chapter 7 (Parallelism)

Week Five
Test Chapters 6 and 7
Chapter 8 (Using Adjectives and Adverbs) and Chapter 9 (Correcting problems With Modifiers)

Week Six
Test Chapters 8 and 9
Chapter 10 (Verbs: The Four Main Forms) and Chapter 11 (Verb Tenses)

Week Seven
Test Chapters 10 and 11
Chapter 12 (Verb Consistency and Voice) and Chapter 13 (Subject-Verb Agreement)

Week Eight
Test Chapters 12 and 13
Chapter 14 (Pronoun Agreement and Reference) and Chapter 15 (Pronouns: Consistency

and Case)
Week Nine
Test Chapters 14 and 15
Chapter 16 (Punctuation)
Test Chapter 16

Week Ten
Chapter 17 (Spelling), Chapter 18 (Words That Sound Alike/ look Alike), and Chapter19 (Using Prepositions Correctly)
Test Chapters 17, 18, and 19

Week Eleven
Chapter 20 (Generating Ideas)
Chapter 21 (Devising a Plan)

Week Twelve
Finish Chapter 21
Chapter 22 (Writing, Revising, and Editing the Draft)

Week Thirteen
Chapter 23 (Polishing, Proofreading, and Preparing the Final Copy)

Week Fourteen
Chapter 24 (Focus on Coherence and Unity)
Chapter 25 (Focus on Support and Details)

Week Fifteen
Finish Chapter 25
Chapter 26 (Writing From Reading)

Week Sixteen
Finish Chapter 26
Paragraphs due
Final Exam Review